12 WORDS

To Jeanie and Martus,
May you always be
blessed by the grace
and peace of our Lord,
Jesus Christ!

Susan Dodson

SUSAN DODSON

ISBN 978-1-64515-734-2 (paperback)
ISBN 978-1-64515-735-9 (digital)

Christian Faith Publishing, Inc.
832 Park Avenue
Meadville, PA 16335
www.christianfaithpublishing.com

Printed in the United States of America

First and foremost, this book is dedicated to my Lord, Jesus Christ. Without Him, there would be no words at all.

Thank you to my husband, Chip, who has faithfully supported me through all my highs and lows. He takes the brunt of my pity parties and the supinity of my awakenings and loves me through them all. There is a special place in heaven for you my love!

To my dad, who has never given up encouraging me to put this book together.

To my pastor, Dr. Scott Sharman, for delivering solid Christian theology and teaching me that there is more to being a Christian than just showing up on Sunday. The Spirit that works through you continues to challenge me to dig deeper.

To my sisters, my mom, and my sisters in Christ who have walked with me through this journey. You know who you are, and you know that I love you dearly!

Introduction

> Sing, O barren woman, you who never bore a child; burst into song, shout for joy, you who were never in labor; because more are the children of the desolate woman, than of her who has a husband. Enlarge the place of your tent, stretch your tent curtains wide, do not hold back; lengthen your cords, strengthen your stakes. For you will spread to the right and to the left; your descendants will dispossess nations and settle in the desolate cities. (Isaiah 54:1–3)[1]

God has been so gracious in bringing purpose out of my pain. He has made something beautiful out of this lonely and barren life and has taught me that my purpose isn't in the lie that my value is based upon having children. But my value lies in Him! I am the daughter of a King! And that makes my life worth living.

I had taken my pain and stuffed it into a bitter world of exclusion. I learned to avoid situations that made me hurt and began to fill that void in my heart with gambling. Soon it was an addiction that consumed my every thought. Gambling had become a hiding place, an identity of sorts, replacing the value in myself I had lost while searching for a purpose to survive.

God exchanged my gambling for his glory just six months after my pastor, Dr. Scott Sharman[2], delivered twelve words in a prayer for a friend. Little did Scott know those words were meant for me. But God knew, and he began to turn them into powerful transformation. Those twelve little words: "Quality of life doesn't depend on the number of kids you have." They were the hope I needed to see

God's plan for my life to begin to unfold. And although His plan didn't include having kids, it gets more beautiful each day as I watch it grow into perfection.

I had known God all my life but had not realized the vibrant beauty of His grace. The comfort of a personal relationship with Him or the power and the purpose that comes from receiving and giving His love.

God's plan would be to seek Him, to trust Him, and to surrender all I have to Him. I can't even begin to comprehend what he has planned for me in the future, as it seems to change every day, but He has given me a direction I would have never chosen for myself. I know the assurance of my eternal destination and am confident that my purpose is to share this same hope with others who are trapped in a path of self-destruction. God doesn't remove our loneliness, pain, or suffering; but he does give us a better way to deal with it.

The devotions in this book are the result of His saving grace. He has inspired me to take my pain and turn it into words of love, hope, joy, and peace. I pray that as you read these words, you too will find a special place in your heart for the goodness and the grace that only God can provide.

12 Words

Gambling promised everything and delivered nothing.
God's promises delivered purpose and peace.

A Million Dollars

The Million Dollar Wall at the Horseshoe Casino[3] draws thousands of people to have their picture taken with one hundred, $10,000 bills! I do have to say, I was intrigued by the value of the money inside the protected walls of this famous tourist attraction and yes, we have our picture tucked away in the memories of our early years.

Money makes us do funny things. We daydream about how we could spend it and get giddy thinking about having more. We hoard it away or pretentiously spend.

But really, money is just a piece of paper waiting to be validated. It has no value in the bill itself. It's not the fiber in the money, the appearance of the money, the essence of the money, or the place we keep it that makes it valuable. It only becomes valuable when, like faith, we use it. It proves itself only when it's real and exchanged for something of worth. And standing in front of a million dollars means nothing but a counterfeit experience of worthiness.

So how do we value our faith? Do we live a faith that is real and valuable to others, or are we living a counterfeit faith that finds worth only on the pages of a book or in a Sunday morning sermon?

Do we label ourselves a Christian thinking that makes us valuable? Or are we willing to allow God to influence others through us? It is so easy to sit behind the walls of protection and expect others to marvel at our greatness. But that is not what God calls us to do! God calls us to be a vessel that overflows with love, sharing the good news and helping those in need. He expects us to get torn, tattered, and dirty as we circulate in our community and the world. We become valuable as we allow the Spirit to enable us in caring and sharing His worth.

We serve what we treasure the most. And what matters is not who we say we are or who others say we are or how much we have in the bank. What matters is how we use what we have. To share His hope. To share His love. To touch those who are in desperate need of a Savior.

There was that time in my life when I allowed money to allure me. Addicted to gambling, I focused on the "high" that money brought me, the excitement of having more, the label that I was a "winner." I spent more money, trying to have more money finding comfort in an endless cycle of meaningless frivolity. But when I found the true nature of Jesus and started living outside the pages of His book, I realized that I had really had nothing at all.

I'm not saying that money is not important, or that we shouldn't be good stewards with what we have. We should! But our wealth is not found in silver or gold. Our wealth is found in a man named Jesus.

> He had no beauty or majesty to attract us to him, nothing in his appearance that we should desire him", yet, "he was pierced for transgressions, he was crushed for our iniquities; the punishment that brought us peace was upon him, and by his wounds we are healed. (Isaiah 53:2b,5)

12 Words

You are validated and redeemed only by the blood of Jesus Christ.

Unyielding Freedom

It was a day unlike any other for me. I was going to meet a stranger for lunch. Now, that may not sound odd to you, but for me, it was uncanny. It was way out of my comfort zone, and something I had always avoided—one on one conversations. What would we talk about? But even more mysterious on this day was why were we meeting? I had rules. And this was not one of them!

It had started off simple. I had been hired to do a job. But then she asked me to meet her for lunch. I can still remember the deep-seated fear of saying yes. But God had been working mightily in my life, and I knew that He was in control. I prayed. He heard. And He responded with a peace that passes any understanding.

We do tend to make our own rules in life. After all, we know who we are. We know our pain, our insecurities, and our vulnerabilities. We hide to protect ourselves. But guess what? God knows all these things too. And sometimes, we must relinquish control to Him to allow Him to do what only He can do. We may not understand why, but God doesn't ask us to understand. He just asks us to trust. He asks us to rely on His guidance. He asks us to obey, sometimes in big ways, and sometimes in small. And here's the deal that is so amazingly awesome; He never makes a mistake!! And when we let Him lead, He will do far more than we could ever imagine.

At the beginning of that day, you couldn't have paid me to think this was God's plan, but by the end of the week, I had been given a gift that only God can provide—freedom.

This meeting for lunch allowed me to surrender pieces of my past to the path that God had for me. I was given the freedom to begin to heal. The freedom to learn how to love in unimaginable ways. The freedom to worship Him in a way I had never understood.

And there is no greater gift I could ask for. My rules kept me well within the walls of my comfort zone. But God stretched me. And when we are stretched, we become flexible to be used in situations that otherwise would be missed.

You see, before that day, I had been saving my wedding dress for a special little girl I had not been able to conceive. But God is able to do immeasurably more than we ask or imagine (Ephesians 3:20), and on this day, I was given the opportunity to donate the dress to a charity that would bless many families over and over. My pain would be used for a comforting peace to many grieving families. But most of all, my fear-driven insecurity would be forever released to be used for God's glory and grace.

This was truly a day that the Lord had made. I will rejoice, be glad, and always be thankful.

What rules do you need to change to become flexible for God?

"O great and powerful God, whose name is Lord Almighty, great are your purposes and mighty are your deeds" (Jeremiah 32:18b-19a).

12 Words

Our rules keep us comfortable, but obedience
stretches us into unyielding freedom.

Artificial Enemies

We had no idea! The old house was so alluring, and our curiosity got the best of us, so we decided to explore. Before we knew it though, there were swarms of bees, buzzing around us protecting their hive. We had no intentions of harm, but as innocent bystanders, we decided it was best to just walk away. The bees and us would have to forever part ways.

Sadly, this is how some of our relationships end as well, because we so easily get offended by others. Sometimes it's something that is unintentionally said or done. Sometimes it's as simple as a misunderstanding. Sometimes it's our own anxious pursuit of how a certain situation might go. Any way we look at it though, our misconstrued notions create artificial enemies and we declare war on innocent bystanders who may never have had intentions to harm us.

I wonder how much time we waste and how many relationships we strain by turning our offense into battles in our minds? And how often are we turned into the offender by fixating on things that others have no idea they did?

Our misconceptions can lead to disaster if we don't keep them in check. Taking offense, and letting it fester, destroys lives. Just like a swarm of bees, our actions can cause others to flee, forever severing ties that could otherwise be repaired.

Let God search your heart and point out areas of offense. Give your anxious thoughts to Him, allowing Him to lead you to reconciliation, and let the peace of Christ rule in your life.

"Search me, O God, and know my heart; test me and know my anxious thoughts. See if there is any offensive way in me and lead me in the way everlasting" (Psalm 139:23).

12 Words

Our artificial enemies are irrationally driven.
Destroy them before they destroy you.

Be Intentional

We live in a time where it is easy to shrink back from society. Social media, online education, email, texts; all these keep us from interacting face to face or voice to voice. It creates an illusion of indifference. Let's face it, people can be difficult to deal with sometimes. It's much easier to be apathetic, rather than allowing ourselves to be vulnerable. Sadly though, as we begin to lose that personal touch with others, we begin to look out only for ourselves. When we are mindful only of ourselves, it is easy to develop a selfish pride. A pride that refuses to rejoice instead of being jealous. A pride that's unwilling to compromise instead of showing hostility. A pride unable to humble ourselves with compassion rather than judge other's situations. A pride unyielding to love instead of scorn. But everyone deserves to be loved, including ourselves! Doing God's work takes intentional effort. And God's work is about people. Find someone today that you can bless with a smile, a hug, or maybe just a quick word of encouragement. Pick up the phone and call your friend. Meet someone for coffee. Talk to that homeless man on the corner. God asks us as believers to be fishers of men. Use your best bait and reel someone in to the blessing of being loved and accepted by you! People may not always remember what you say, but they will remember how you made them feel.

"Be wise in the way you act toward outsiders; make the most of every opportunity" (Colossians 4:5).

12 Words

Let go of yourself and intentionally be available
for personal, meaningful connections.

Joyful Hope

"Be joyful in hope, patient in affliction, and faithful in prayer" (Romans 12:12). Whether it's a family member that's gone astray, an unexpected illness, a paycheck that doesn't seem to stretch far enough, a decision that needs to be made, or an unmerciful disease that invades your body, it really is possible to be joyful, patient, and faithful in prayer.

Joy is defined by an emotion of great delight caused by something exceptionally good or satisfying[4]. It may seem hard to find joy in the midst of those things that don't seem so good. But Christ promises to satisfy our every need. He is exceptionally good, and we can celebrate in the hope of what is to come. We can have joy and take great delight in spite of our circumstances, because we know this hope does not disappoint us or put us to shame. This hope pours God's love into our hearts so we can be joyful with praise and thanksgiving.

Patience. Yes, this is a hard one. Quiet, steady perseverance, even-tempered care, suppression of complaint or loss of temper due to annoyance, misfortune or pain[5]. When we focus on God, rather than on our stressful situations, He will bring us the patience we need to keep our emotions from consuming us. When we patiently endure in faith, knowing that the blessings of comfort, healing, and hope come only from our Father, we begin to understand what is not yet understood. We strengthen our relationship with our Lord as we see His faithfulness sustain us in peace through our times of trouble.

Faithful in prayer. Steady, affectionate, and loyal.[6] Pray with all your heart. Not as a patient to a doctor or a master to a genie. But as a loving child to your almighty, loving Father. God is your greatest help, and He wants to walk beside you intimately. He wants to heal your heart and your mind, bringing you into a place of perfect peace. His answers may not be what we want or when we want them, but He works everything out for our good. He may be teaching you lessons to use for greater purposes in the future, so never give up. Be faithful in prayer, get to know Him, and take notice as you see His plans unfold.

God may not free you from your unfortunate circumstances, but He may instead free you from yourself, molding you into a masterpiece that will shine His light in the darkest of times. Be joyful. Be patient. Be faithful in prayer.

12 Words

Be joyful. Be patient. Be prayerful. While
you're waiting, God is working.

The Anaconda Truth

As I was scrolling through Facebook one day, I saw a picture of the world's largest snake[7]. An Anaconda weighing in at 4,556 pounds and measuring 134 feet long had recently been found. This picture made me stop and think; could this really be true? As I looked at the picture, it looked real. And the people standing around it looked real. But I had to discern if I thought this was the truth.

It is often difficult to know what the truth really is. We live in a world of technology where photos can be altered and interviews can be modified. Words are manipulated. People pretend to be something they are not to impress others. And lies and greed are the basis of worth and power. The truth is always changing, depending on who you talk with or listen to.

But there is one truth that has been around for thousands of years—the Word of God. Many people stop and think; could this really be true? How can it be logical? They doubt because it is too mysterious and too hard to understand! But it's really very simple; The Word of God has not changed, but many lives *have* been changed by the Word of God. Courageous, strong, and stubborn men witnessed the miracles of Christ two thousand years ago, but their doubts kept them blinded to who He really was. And it wasn't until they personally witnessed His resurrection that they believed. Once they believed, their lives began to move from misery to hope. Changed hearts don't lie. They cannot be altered or modified. They cannot be manipulated or pretend to be something else. Changed lives are powerful and truthful testimonies to the unchanging Living Word of God.

The Word brings power to change what happens in our heart. And once our hearts are changed, we'll never doubt where the truth is found again. Jesus is "the Way, the Truth, and the Life" (John

14:6). Let God teach you His truth and see the power of transformation that takes place, not only in you, but in how you see the world around you.

"Show me your ways, O Lord, teach me your paths; guide me in your truth and teach me, for you are God my savior, and my hope is in you all day long" (Psalm 25:4–5).

12 Words

God's truth is bigger and better than you or I can imagine.

Beauty is in the Eye of our Beholder

Beauty is in the eye of the beholder. As humans, we tend to strive for outward perfection and work hard to fix the image that we see. Often though, we can get so caught up trying to fix what we see, that we cover up our inner beauty of being created in God's image.

Start this day by taking a few minutes to look in the mirror. Look beyond the immediate image for the reflection of God our Father and Creator. Ask Him to help you recognize the inward perfection of who you are and seek His advice on enhancing touch-ups. Highlight His attributes by cleansing your heart, contouring your mind, and unmasking your soul. Most of all, be confident that when you see yourself, and other's look at you, what's seen is God and His radiant beauty shining bright.

"Man looks at outward appearance, but the Lord looks at the heart" (1 Samuel 16:7).

12 Words

He is our Beholder! He is our Perfecter! And you are beautiful!

But God

But God? But God!

God calls us to do things that can be very uncomfortable. He will purposely use the most unlikely candidates for a job or a service that he wants done. He may ask us to do something really big, or it may be the smallest of things. But how often do we accept his challenge? How often do we let doubt and fear cloud our faith and make excuses for why we can't?

But God? How can I do that? I don't have time. I just don't know enough. There's not enough people to help. It's way too hard. You want me to give that up? Are you crazy, God? I just can't! But thank you, Lord, maybe next time!

When we make excuses why we can't do something, we are denying ourselves the blessing of God's guidance and direction. God will never ask us to do something that He is not willing to walk us through. And when we are willing to let God help us, we can accept any assignment with confidence that it will be completed to the fullest. We must be willing to let God help us use our gifts for His purpose. No task is too hard when we are powered by God.

But God! You made it possible! You provided time and resources. You instilled the knowledge. You made it seem so easy! Thank you, Lord. You *are* enough!

Next time you want to make that clever excuse for not doing something, instead ask God for his help. You will be amazed at what we see as impossible is always possible with God!

But God? But God!

"Jesus looked at them and said, 'With man this is impossible, but with God all things are possible'" (Matthew 19:26).

12 Words

Our greatest challenge is letting go and letting God make it happen!

Love Never Fails

Love can be the hardest thing to do sometimes. It's the greatest commandment, yet it's the one that we seem to get so wrong so often. There's a song that goes, "And they'll know we are Christians by our love, by our love."[8] I hear that, and I wonder how effective we really are as Christians. How effective am I?

> Love is patient, love is kind. It does not envy. It does not boast, it is not proud. It is not rude, it is not self-seeking, it is not easily angered, it keeps no record of wrongs. Love does not delight in evil but rejoices with the truth. It always protects, always trusts, always hopes, always perseveres. (1 Corinthians 13:4–7)

God doesn't put conditions on His love. He doesn't ask us to love only if someone meets our expectations. He doesn't ask us to love only if we see eye to eye. He doesn't ask us to love only if we feel warm and fuzzy today. No, God asks us to love in all circumstances. God's greatest commandment is love because He doesn't delight in conflict. He delights in peace. He asks us to love because it is our testimony of Jesus and the way to show others His truth. If we can't love unconditionally, we can't fully be the light of Christ.

Love never fails. It can turn the worst of situations into an opportunity for peace. Don't hold yourself to a higher standard than the one you choose to judge. Instead, make love count today. It will not only make you feel better, but it may just be the beginning of a beautiful friendship.

"And now these three remain: faith, hope, and love, but the greatest of these is love" (1 Corinthians 13:13).

12 Words

Your greatest influence on others is the way you make them feel.

Chrysanthemums[9]

Chrysanthemums, if pruned correctly and at the right time, will blossom into beautiful and mature plants. They can be the healthy result of good soil but need to be watered and fertilized regularly to continue to abundantly grow. It takes planning and work on our part, but only God determines when it will bloom.

We tend to want to go against nature though and plan without allowing God time to work. We want to do things our way and in our own time. But when we submit everything we do to the Lord, He will successfully grow the fruits of our efforts. When we trust God and acknowledge that everything depends on Him, instead of acting like everything depends on us, our plans begin to flourish.

As you go into this day, commit your ways to the Lord. Ask God for a new commitment to plant seeds of His grace in everything you do. Ask for opportunities to be pruned by God so that no one misses His grace. Ask how you can help those in your sphere of influence to bloom into the beautiful people God intends for them to be. And ask Him for patience in all that you do, making your actions and words be pleasing to Him so your plans, in His time, will grow fruit for generations to come.

"Commit to the Lord whatever you do, and your plans will succeed"(Proverbs 16:3, NLT).

12 Words

Don't move ahead of God. Trust Him to finish what He started.

Weekend Coupons

The Sunday morning paper has always been exciting to me because it has coupons! And who doesn't want to save, right? The less it costs me, the better it is. Some have savings of a few cents, but BOGOs are the best! Buy one get one free! We can get a whole lot for a little bit of nothing.

Often times though, the value of the coupon actually becomes costlier to me because I find myself using it on something I really didn't think I needed. I use the coupon, well, because, it looks like a good deal. But other times, I find that item useful, so it becomes a staple to my list, and I continue to buy it at full price.

When I think about our relationship with Christ, I think about my coupons. We tend to want a whole lot for a little bit of nothing. We take for granted that Jesus paid everything for us, and we are so quick to sell Him short. We take the gift that He so freely gives us and return it with as little sacrifice as possible. We have become accustomed to cheap grace[10]. We have become complacent with our own reason. We have become selfish and keep as much for ourselves as we can. We offer him our leftovers. We want our treasure hidden in the field, our nets full of fish, and our fine pearls of heaven, but we want it at the cheapest price possible.

It is so easy to accept that ticket to heaven, but it's not so easy to pay the price by living a righteous life. Jesus' grace is so amazing! And He offers it to us at no cost. We can take it anytime, but oh how much more we could afford?

What keeps you from paying full price for His grace? Is it bitterness, or anger, or fear? Is it control, or power, or greed?

Jesus' value will not change. He is the same today, tomorrow, and forever. When we allow ourselves to find His Word useful and start applying it to our lives, even if we think we don't need it, our lives will change. Our relationships will change. Our character will change. Our hearts will change. What we are willing to give back to Him will increase. Not because He expects it but because we want to!

I do look forward to my Sunday coupons. But I've learned that my greatest value is the treasures I find in knowing Jesus. The comfort I find in His presence. The fulfillment I find in a relationship with Him. My greatest value is the priceless love of my Father. He gave his life so we could have eternal life. What is the cost you are willing to pay for His grace?

"Live as free men, but do not use your freedom as a cover-up for evil; live as servants of God" (1 Peter 2:16).

12 Words

Don't let His free gift keep you from investing more for Him.

Dare to be Different

Do not conform any longer to the pattern of this world but be transformed by the renewing of your mind. Then you will be able to test and approve what God's will is - his good, pleasing, and perfect will. (Romans 12:2)

As you read this verse, be thankful that God is a God of patience and grace. Be thankful that no challenge is too hard for Him, and that He doesn't give up on you! Be thankful too that you will never achieve His perfection until you sit at His feet on His throne. When you fail to meet His perfection on earth, let it bring you closer to him. Let it take you to your knees in repentance and develop a new determination to surrender your stubborn and selfish ways. It will be uncomfortable sometimes, but when you embrace what He wants for your life, you'll be able to see His amazing grace and allow His Spirit to begin yet another good work in you. When you recognize how much you get for what you don't deserve, you'll only love Him more.

Ask God today to reveal to you his good, pleasing, and perfect will. Ask Him what you need to surrender to be different. Different than you are now. Different to the world. Different for His kingdom. Be patient, be thankful, and be open to His grace.

12 Words

Dare to be different. Let God begin His good work in you.

Freely Give

Freely, I have been given. Freely, I will give. In freedom, I will live. I am blessed! Yes, God has been good to me. He has given me many tangible things—a roof over my head, clothes on my back, the means to pay my bills. These are all good things.

But it's the intangible things that bring me true fortune. It's the unconditional devotion of my husband. The unexpected call from a friend at just the right time. Being greeted with a kiss of love. The celestial power to make what I think is impossible, possible. The love of a man to give His life for my dirty rotten sin.

There are many blessings to receive. And because God never holds back His blessings, even when things aren't so great, we can praise Him still. He gives us strength to carry on. Comfort to uphold us. Power, protection, and purpose. Undeserved grace.

Neither should we hold back from Him. We should stand in front of Him and say *yes* because He takes our hopelessness and turns it into promise. Even in my darkest days, He blesses me with His glorious presence. I don't hope anymore that God can. No, because I know that He will!

Today, remember the freedom we've been given through Christ and commit to freely give of yourself as you have so freely been given.

"Give as freely as you have received" (Matthew 10:8b, NLT).[11]

12 Words

Giving is evidence of God's blessing. Give generously. Serve passionately. Love fearlessly.

Significant

Significant. That's a pretty big word. Webster defines it as: import-ant; worthy of attention; the meaning to be found in events or words; observations that are unlikely to occur by chance.[12]

Our lives often change in an instant and our plans can be redi-rected without our permission. We find it hard to understand why things happen the way they do and get sidetracked by fear, frustra-tion, and selfishness.

When I broke my foot several years ago, it really wasn't anything special to anyone else. But to me it was a big deal. It was right before the holidays and ten weeks out from my first mission trip. I could say at the time that this inconvenience really shook me to the core. I didn't under-stand the timing of it, and it was something I was going to have to wait out. And being short on patience, waiting was not an option for me. I wanted to control how fast I would heal. I wanted to get my Christmas shopping done. I wanted to go to parties. And I wanted assurance that I would go on my mission trip. But most of all, I wanted to be able to walk. Being slow was not in my nature, and this really slowed me down.

As I look back now and am adjusting to a new normal of living with Lupus, I see that breaking my foot was really one of the best things that could have happened to me. Because even though I didn't get my Christmas shopping done, I missed most of my parties, I waited nine weeks before I was able to walk again, and I didn't get to go on my mission trip for other reasons, I did grow stronger in my faith. I built a closer relationship with God. I learned a lot of patience. And I had to let go of control. All of these prepared me for what I'm facing today.

We may never understand why things happen the way they do. But our hardships could cause us to see something that we otherwise might have missed. The times in our life when we must try the hardest to see the good are usually the times that God shows up in a big way. We must let go of our control, be patient, and let Him work. And be fully aware of His significance every single day.

For me, I saw God's faithfulness through my selfishness. I saw God's mercy through my impatience. But most of all, I saw God's bigness in my little corner of this world. He is all powerful, all present, and all knowing. He cares for his most valuable creations—you and me. He is mighty, and when we take note of His incomprehensible details, we find order and beauty, love and forgiveness, mercy and grace.

Had I not paid attention and stayed focused on His Word during this time, I may have very well missed the blessing of His plan. Instead of feeling sorry for ourselves and asking why things are happening, we should see our hardships as an opportunity to grow closer to God. He loves you and cares for you and wants only the best for you.

"How precious to me are your thoughts, O God! How vast is the sum of them! Were I to count them, they would outnumber the grains of sand" (Psalm 139:17–18).

12 Words

What God is teaching you today will be
your strength for tomorrow.

Desperate Measures

Desperate times call for desperate measures. A saying we use when we are in a tough situation and we'll do anything to make it better. We may put this into action when money is tight and we must find that second job, or when our kids are being knuckleheads and it's time for tough love.

All too often, this is how we pattern our prayer life as well. We go through the motions of our hectic lives not giving a thought about prayer until something bad happens. Then we desperately call on our Father to help make our time of need better.

But God is available for a consistent and faithful relationship with us, and unlike us, His circumstances do not change. *He* is unchangeable! Our prayers are not a tool to be used only in our time of need. Our prayers should be persistent and always intended to bring Him glory.

When we are not in dire need, we might find it hard to really know *what* to pray or even *how* to pray. But the truth is, all you really need to know is Him! When you open your heart and cry out to God, His Spirit will intercede in accordance to His will (Romans 8:27). You will find spiritual wisdom and understanding and begin to see the needs of the world as God sees them.

The prayers of the faithful are found throughout the Bible, and when you turn to the truth of His Word, you find the truth of His love, which brings inspiration of what and how to pray. As you begin to consistently pray and pattern your prayers for His kingdom, God begins to change you! Then when the desperate times come, you find comfort knowing that He is already there! Your problems may not disappear, but your desperation becomes more about how the result can glorify Him and less about your discomfort. When your perspective changes, you can meet the world with an enduring power and greet your Father with faithful patience, being able to be joyful and giving thanks in peaceful *and* desperate times.

> For this reason, since the day we heard about you, we have not stopped praying for you and asking God to fill you with the knowledge of his will through all spiritual wisdom and understanding. And we pray this in order that you may live a life worthy of the Lord and may please him in every way; bearing fruit in every good work, growing in the knowledge of God, being strengthened with all power according to his glorious might so that you may have great endurance and patience, and joyfully giving thanks to the Father, who has qualified you to share in the inheritance of the saints in the kingdom of light. (Colossians 1:9–12)

12 Words

Let your prayers help you live your life with a new perspective.

Be Happy

Don't worry be happy![13] We've all heard that phrase, and now, you'll be singing that song in your head the rest of the day! And I hope you do my friends! A good laugh and a good song does the heart well! It keeps you young and brightens your days. But laughing itself won't take away the anxiety that distresses your heart.

"Do not be anxious about anything, but instead pray about everything." When God is the core of your existence, you can praise Him! Even when things are not so happy. When we set aside time for meaningful and intentional prayer, we not only begin to feel peace about our situations, but we also begin to hear the heart of God. God wants us to come to Him, not only for our own needs but also for the needs of others. Ask Him to fill you with His will, and as we begin to pray prayers that are focused on His kingdom, rather than prayers that are focused only on us, our worries begin to dissipate into joyful songs of praise.

"If God is for us, who can be against us?" (Romans 8:31b). The battle is His, not ours. He's just waiting for us to come to Him, to seek his kingdom first, and trust Him with the details. Instead of worrying, be thankful! And pray! What a wonderful gift it is to approach your Father in prayer. He alone will replace your distress with the peace that passes all understanding. If we will only be a warrior instead of a worrier.

> Don't worry about anything; instead pray about everything. Tell God what you need and thank him for all he has done. Then you will experience God's peace, which exceeds anything we can understand. His peace will guard your hearts and

minds as you live in Christ Jesus. (Philippians 4:6–7, NLT)

12 Words

Worry not; trust a lot. Be happy in the presence of God.

Go!

Preparing for the big game can be tireless. I imagine before a football game, as the teams are getting ready to play, they have a lot going on in their minds. Each is preparing for victory! They must have the proper gear and a balanced mind to protect themselves from injury and defeat their opponent; both are equally important. Even those sitting on the sidelines are expected to play when the coach says go.

The same is true for our spiritual lives. God doesn't ask us to be spectators on the sidelines of life. He asks us to go. The best thing is we don't have to be professionals or have specific training. He gives us all that we need to be ready and defeat our opponent. The belt of Truth. The breastplate of righteousness. The footgear of readiness. The shield of faith. The helmet of Salvation. The sword of the Spirit.

We are all on the roster to be drafted. We are all worthy to *go*. We just have to say *yes*! Are you a spectator or an active player? Will you shine up your armor and calibrate your gear? Don't just sit on the sidelines; be a part of the action! Go! Make disciples and prepare for victory.

"All authority in heaven has been given to me. Therefore, go and make disciples of all the nations" (Matthew 28:18b–19a).

12 Words

What does the Gospel, Good News and God have in common? *Go!*

The Grand Canyon

I had made it to the edge trying my best to muster up the courage to move forward. I had, for years, wanted to see the Grand Canyon, and I was finally there. But my fear of heights got the best of me. I could not make myself do it. I just knew that if I stepped any closer, I would go tumbling into the gorge below.

How foolish was I to allow my imagination and my fear to prevail above all reason or logic! There clearly were sturdy rails that were set in stone, and I'm pretty sure that millions of people had stood in that very same place. But I was stubborn and was not going to move.

Finally though, through much patient and loving encouragement from my husband who, I might add, had driven me 1,047 miles to see this very place, I took a step forward to enjoy the beauty of the abyss before me.

God's Word can seem unreasonable, and He is often misrepresented. And even though we can see the rails of safety and the stones of stability, we let our fear of the unknown drive us away. We can't make sense of it, so we overlook it for more pleasurable pastimes. And after all, His Words were written over two thousand years ago. A lot has changed since then.

But just as the rain continues to transform the earth into beautiful green pastures before it evaporates back to the sky, His Word continues to transform us into His image. It has been around for over two thousand years; yet, it has not changed. His Word remains the same and His love remains the same. The transforming power that is found in His Word accomplishes what He desires and achieves the purpose for which He sent it. It is meant to grow us, encourage us, strengthen us, and bring us into a purposeful life of glory for Him.

It is not meant to harm us, but to bring us a good future filled with hope.

God is very patient, and there is no need to be afraid. Scripture is not about what you can't do. It's about what you can do! The unimaginable things you can do through the power of His Word. He will bring you the desire to love Him above all reason or logic, the understanding to apply it and live in His image, the courage to trust him with the absence of fear, and the hope of life everlasting. Lean upon Him, your Rock and Redeemer. Take that next step forward. And there you'll find God's glorious beauty and be led forth in peace.

> My word is like the snow and the rain that come down from the sky to water the earth. They make the crops grow and provide seed for sowing and food to eat. So, also will be the word that I speak — it will not fail to do what I plan for it; it will do everything I send it to do. "You will leave Babylon with joy; you will be led out of the city in peace. The mountains and hills will burst into singing, and the trees will shout for joy. Cypress trees will grow where now there are briars; myrtle trees will come up in place of thorns. This will be a sign that will last forever, a reminder of what I, the Lord, have done." (Isaiah 55:10–13 GNB)[14]

12 Words

Don't focus on what you can't do but what God's Power can.

World Peace

I don't believe in coincidence. I believe that everything happens for a reason and that God is always at work. When we see His presence in everything we do, we can't deny that it's something greater than just the occurrence of chance. I haven't always believed this way. But I've learned that most of my "coincidences" have turned out to be lessons from my wise and loving Father.

As I was growing up, and even until a few years ago, I found it so coincidental that when I needed some comfort, I could just open my Bible randomly, and God would bring me a verse that I needed to hear! I would get so excited, say thank you, Lord, then get on with my life. My quick Bible fix could bring me instant gratification, but it didn't bring me peace, purpose, and resolution. It wasn't until I found myself hopeless and helpless that I was able to begin to appreciate the life changing power of His words and instructions.

In this world today, we find ourselves hopeless and helpless. We want to change the world! We want to fight for world peace! And we want to matter! But it's not up to us to make those things happen. There is only one way to simply find peace in this world. That is through Jesus Christ. He is the truth, the way and the life, and our confident assurance of the peaceful world to come.

I pray that our hearts will be satisfied, not with the world as it is today, but by the One who came into this world to save us from this world.

My prayer for you today is that you make choices that are pleasing and glorifying to God. I pray that you can set aside your own agendas and concentrate on God's agenda. I pray that His fulfilling grace is understood and accepted by you today, and through Him, you will find peace, assurance, hope, and salvation.

For God so loved the world that he gave he his one and only Son, that whoever believes in him shall not perish but have everlasting life. For God did not send his Son to condemn the world, but to save the world through him. (John 3:16–17)

12 Words

God's Word was not written by chance. It all points to Jesus.

Grandma's Iris

Every year, I look forward to seeing the Iris bloom in my flower bed. My Grandma had abundant beds of these perennials, which continued to multiply over the years into thousands of blooming beards all over her yard. After her passing, as I wept, I took little pieces of her garden with me. Now, Grandma's Iris, continue to bloom in *my* backyard, as delightfully and beautifully as they did fifty years ago, bringing me a harvest full of joy and many fond memories.

As I sit in reflection of the pains of loss, I am quickly reminded of the beauty of the cross. I think of the sorrow that surrounded Jesus' journey and the grief that he and his followers felt. How often do we ask God, just as Jesus did, to take this cup from us?

Just as God did not answer Jesus' prayer by relieving him of His suffering, He does not always answer ours either. Grief is a fact of life, but it doesn't have to be a permanent condition. Our grief, if we allow it to, will point us to the cross.

In Jeremiah 31:13, the Lord says, "I will turn their mourning into gladness; I will give them comfort and joy instead of sorrow." God desires to comfort us and to bring us joy in our sadness. He will respond when we ask for His help. But amid our sorrow, we often tend to blame Him and question why instead.

If we carefully look though, we will see Him lovingly drawing us near. Christ's death was necessary for us to fully live. He suffered on the cross so we don't have to. And if we allow His love to consume us, His joy will consume us also.

So instead of asking God to take this cup, ask how He can fill it. Ask Him for little pieces of hope. For little seeds of joy. Ask Him to grow your grief into something more beautiful than you could ever imagine.

And just as the Iris brings me joy in remembrance of my grandma, the cross will bring you joy in the depths of your sorrow. I pray that you can look beyond your grief today and find the beauty of the joy to follow. "Weeping may endure for the night, but joy comes in the morning!" (Psalm 30:5, NKJV)[15]

12 Words

There's joy beyond sadness and healing
behind grief. Look to the Cross!

Jesus, our Carpenter

> Therefore everyone who hears these words of
> mine and puts them into practice is like a wise
> man who built his house on the rock. The rain
> came down, the streams rose, and the winds blew
> and beat against the house: yet it did not fall,
> because its foundation was built upon the rock.
> (Matthew 7:24–25)

This verse brings back memories from my days at Meadowbrook
Baptist Church where I learned that Jesus was a carpenter. With
my Dad being a very talented woodworker, always in his woodshop
whipping out one thing or another; my mind's eye as a child, envisioned Jesus doing the same. Not since I was a child, have I really
given much thought to Jesus being a carpenter.

As I search the Bible today, there is not much mention about
His physical carpentry work. Not a word on the kind of house he
built for himself to live in or how he provided for himself. Instead,
there is evidence of Him constructing lives for the kingdom. He
taught, He encouraged, He healed, He served, He loved. He died
on a cross to build our stairway to heaven. Jesus is the very rock
on which we build our lives. The blueprints have been drawn up
for us with Christ as the foundation and the Center Stone. Will we
choose to build our house on a firm foundation that will survive any
storm that comes our way? Or will we reject the stone and follow our
own selfish desires, building our future on sand that washes away?

Our spiritual home awaits us if we will only allow Jesus to be our carpenter!

12 Words

He chose nails and a wooden cross to build our eternal home.

Computer Lit

I remember the day when my vocational counselor registered me for computer literature classes. It was my senior year, and she insisted that computers were the thing of the future. I fought it tooth and nail because I didn't see any need for this big bulky machine.

I know now she was right! You couldn't have paid me then to even think we would carry around little computers everywhere we go! Our phones have become an extension of ourselves. It has everything we need to keep us on track. We can find out anything we need to know with the push of a button. We even carry around power cords to make sure we don't miss a thing.

We cannot imagine depriving ourselves of this powerful connection to the world. It brings simplicity and efficiency to our daily routines. But all too often, this connection, in turn, ends up depriving us of our real identity—our identity in Christ. We get so caught up in texting, social media, emails, and working from the palm of our hands that we forget who it is who holds us in the palm of His hand.

The truth is the one who holds us *is* the provider of everything we need. He is omnipotent. He is omnipresent. He is omniscient. His power is great and will never run out. His presence surrounds us and will never desert us. His knowledge is unlimited and will never lead us astray.

And think about how much time we spend searching our phones for answers and connecting with people we haven't seen in years. It is no wonder that we tend to crave that little gadget. But what if we had that same thirst for God? What if we relied upon Him, instead of our phones, to satisfy our desire for more?

We may not really see a need for God in our lives. After all, we have all that we could ever want in that little computer we carry around. But God is the most we will ever need. He is our strength and our shield. His unlimited resources and knowledge far exceeds anything a computer could ever begin to process. And when we accept His friend request, He will not only be the best friend we ever have, He will be our friend for eternity.

Today, you might try to turn off your phone. Don't just silence it. Turn it off. Choose Jesus as your friend. Sit, communicate, and receive His love. Receive His knowledge. Receive His companionship. And trust Him. Trust that He is enough, because He alone, is the One who holds our future!

"So we fix our eyes not on what is seen, but on what is unseen. For what is seen is temporary, but what is unseen is eternal" (2 Corinthians 4:18).

12 Words

Jesus is infinitely better than anything this world has to offer us.

Kingdom Courage

The day had come that I was going to return what I had stolen. I was scared to death not knowing how I would be punished, but the nagging in my mind and the aching of my heart was more than I could take. I was in kindergarten and had stolen a toy clown from my class. I can't quite say why I stole it, other than it was a fun little clown with flexible arms and legs that could bend any which way but loose. I'm sure my parents would have bought me a similar clown, but for some reason, I decided to sneak it out of class and take it home.

And that's when it all began. I couldn't sleep at night! I couldn't look my teacher, or even my parents in the eye. I had to hide this treasured toy and could only play with it by myself because if anyone saw it, they'd know I had stolen it. I was paranoid all the time! Yes, at the ripe old age of five, I was a thief! And I was being taught a precious lesson. At the time, it was a lesson of right and wrong. Looking back on it, forty-two years later, I realize how God was teaching me to listen to His still, small voice of love.

God has a plan for each one of us. He knew His plan while we were still in the womb. But the choices we make can keep us from fulfilling His plan. Sometimes we realize this. Sometimes we don't. But His still, small voice is always prompting us to make the right decisions. And when we hear His voice, it takes a lot of courage to take the steps we need to take to follow the path that He is leading.

When He asks us to follow Him, He brings us power, but He also brings us courage. And His courage is motivated by love. When we obey the convictions of our hearts and rely on His strength, our lives are changed, and our hearts are set free to love without fear. Getting rid of the obstacles that keep us from freely loving others, helps us to live the life that God calls us to live. His courage takes us beyond what we think is possible and far exceeds our expectations.

There may be things in your life that you need courage to face. You may need courage to forgive or courage to apologize. You may need to admit that you were wrong to reconcile a relationship. You may need to confess something that is causing your heart to ache and your mind to go crazy! Or you may need courage just to love the person who seems unlovable. These things not only constantly nag at your soul, but they separate you from others and they separate you from God.

Whatever it is that is keeping you in the battlefield, ask God for the courage to do what's right. Even if it harms your pride a little. He will keep you strong. He will restore your soul. He will reward you with peace and joy!

As you begin to draw strength from Him, pay attention to the changes going on inside. It doesn't get easier to find the courage, but it becomes easier to trust that He will love you in spite of your wrongs. And as He does this for us, we find it easier to do this for others.

When I returned the clown, I took it to my teacher, and I told her what I had done. And guess what? She didn't punish me—she thanked me! She thanked me for my honesty and for returning what rightly belonged to the school. All those hours I spent in agony knowing that what I had done was wrong and worrying about how I would be punished turned into a moment of rejoicing. Not only had I cleared my conscious, but I learned that God's justice isn't just about rules, regulations, and punishment. God's justice is about love. He gave me kingdom courage to do what was right and in return I received not only a good night's sleep but a peaceful mind and a joyous heart.

"My strength will always be with him, my power will make him strong. I will love him and be loyal to him; I will make him always victorious" (Psalm 89:21, 24, GNB).

12 Words

Kingdom courage empowers you to do it
afraid. Take God's fearless hand.

Lean Not

As I sat on the plane back from Atlanta, I cried. And these words just kept repeating in my mind; lean not on your own understanding. I had prepared for months for my first mission trip to Haiti! Praying that my broken foot would be healed enough to allow sufficient mobility, I had also prepared spiritually and emotionally for a journey into the unknown. When I got the call that my father-in-law was seriously ill, I'll be honest, I selfishly thought *no*. I'm not turning back. But after seeking wisdom through prayer, I made the decision to return. Even though I don't regret that decision for a minute, it didn't make it easy! After I landed in Dallas, I texted my friend but had not discussed what I had been thinking. Her response to me was this: "Lean not on your own understanding." This was confirmation to me that I had made the right decision. Even though I still didn't understand, I knew it was the right thing to lean on God and not try to understand.

Things don't always work out for us the way we plan them to work out. Unexpected things happen to us every single day; some things are small, and some things are big. And we can waste so much time dwelling on the way we had planned for them to go, regretting the disappointing interruptions and weeping over things that could have been. But God asks us to trust Him with them all—to acknowledge Him in all our ways and let Him make our paths straight. Instead of weeping, we should be seeking. Seeking God's providence in the middle of it all.

Ask God today for His guidance in all that you do. Acknowledge that His ways are better than your ways, and even if you don't understand them, pay close attention remembering that He wants only what is best for you.

"Trust in the Lord with all your heart and lean not on your own understanding; in all your ways acknowledge him, and he will make your paths straight" (Proverbs 3:5–6).

12 Words

God's sovereign providence is embedded in every disappointment. Seek Him. Trust Him.

Our Lost Lighthouse

Life can throw us around like a ship in the dark stormy sea. We wander aimlessly going from one place to the next without an anchor. Our priorities become jumbled and, in our busyness, our vision becomes so foggy we can't see the lighthouse that guides us safely to shore.

In John 8:12, Jesus said, "I am the light of the world. Whoever follows me will never walk in darkness but will have the light of life."

Take a few minutes today to focus on the Light of the world. Give your worries to Him and trust Him to lead the way. Let Him help you to clearly see your priorities. He is your protection and your guide; His light will steer you calmly ashore, where you can drop your anchor with the assurance that you are on rock-solid ground.

12 Words

Seeking the Light of the World will point to the solid Rock.

A Fragrant Testimony

Not only is the Magnolia tree characterized by its beautiful white blossoms, but its fragrance is distinctive and attractive. We too should have a distinctive blossom and attractive fragrance that reflects the grace and the love of Christ. One of the most powerful testimonies we can share is how we present ourselves as Christians to the world around us. Take time today to think before you act, to pray before you speak, to discern before you judge, diffusing the fragrance of Christ to all whom you encounter.

"For we are to God the pleasing aroma of Christ among those who are being saved and those who are perishing" (2 Corinthians 2:15).

12 Words

Be rational, pleasant, authentic. Your behavior
is your testimony to your faith.

Finding Your Stones

His name was Marcelus Hilaire. I met him in Haiti, not once but twice! He had been hobbling around in a full leg cast when I first met him. He had nothing but an old, beat up walker to shuffle around with. You see, in Haiti, medical care doesn't come free. And most of the time, it doesn't come at all. When Marcelus was hit by a rock, breaking his leg, he went to several hospitals only to be turned down. Finally, because of a friend, one month and a half later, he was able to catch a ride to a hospital several hours away. Of course, the bone had already begun to heal even though it was not aligned with the rest of his tibia. But the cast was placed anyway, and he was sent on his way.

He had endured the grueling heat for seven months being trapped in this stone cast when I first met him at the clinic with the hopes of getting it removed. I thought I would never see him again, until we ran across his home three days later in the village fifteen miles away. And there he was, lying in bed on the porch of his cinder-block home. No electricity—only little square vents for windows. No plumbing or water—just an outhouse and wood burning stove. His cast had been removed at the clinic, but his flesh lay hard and chafed. And yes, his tibia was still grossly misaligned. Yet, this seventy-seven-year old man had a heart of gold. His life hadn't been much to tell about, but his faith in God was enormous. He didn't have much to call his own, but He had His Lord and Savior. Marcelus had a story to tell! Not a story of poverty and oppression. But a story of love and victory. And he didn't hesitate sharing it with us.

In Joshua 4, after God stopped the flow of water in the Jordan so the Israelites could cross on dry ground, He asked them to pick up stones as a reminder of this miracle. God asked them to share this story with generations to come so they would always know the power of His hand. So they would always remember His love for them.

Marcelus certainly had stones! The Lord may not have stopped the flow of water so he could cross on dry land, but the Lord had taken his dry life and made it something to celebrate. Marcelus picked up His stones along the way and carried them with him. God didn't bring him wealth or miraculous health, but He brought him the fullness of His presence. God brought Marcelus joy and comfort through a relationship with Him. He provided for him with a roof over his head and enough food to nourish his family. And even though it was not the abundant and comfortable lives we consider a blessing here in America, Marcelus saw the miracle of the Cross. He saw the powerful hand and the love of God each and every day. He was a blessed man! And he knew it!

We too have stories to tell. Although, when we walk through dry land, we tend to forget the raging seas that are behind us. We focus on our current situations and forget God's faithfulness of the past. Today I challenge you to pick up your stones. Dig deep into the rivers of the past and find the stones that helped you cross. His unseen footprints lay embedded deep in your hearts. Set aside the America in you to find what Jesus has done for you. Pick up your stones and praise God. Thank Him. Cherish Him. And tell your story!

Joshua 4:21–24 He said to the sons of Israel,

> When your children ask their fathers in time to come, 'What do those stones mean?' then you shall let your children know, 'Israel crossed this Jordan on dry ground.' For the Lord your God dried up the waters of the Jordan for you until you crossed over, just as the Lord your God did to the Red Sea, which He dried up before us until we had crossed; so that all the peoples of the earth may know [without any doubt] and acknowledge that the hand of the Lord is mighty and extraor-

dinarily powerful, so that you will fear the Lord your God [and obey and worship Him with pro-found awe and reverence] forever. (AMP)[16]

12 Words

Find your hidden stones! They are the parted seas for the future.

Marginal Prayers

William D. Barney once wrote, "At times, reading a book, I discover that I'm doing no such thing, but have drifted off the margin."[17] This can be true in our prayers too. How often have we sat down to pray and suddenly realized that we have wandered off the margins? Suddenly, our to-do list is flashing through our minds as we passively bow our heads in idle thought, instead of reverently bowing to the Creator of Heaven and Earth?

Prayer is something that can be done at all times (Ephesians 6:18) or in communion with others (Acts 4:24) to request God's powerful influence. But it should also be done on a regular basis alone with God. Just as Jesus regularly got away for quiet time with His Father, we too, should intentionally set aside time for deep, reflective, relational prayer.

But don't be too quick to tell God our struggles and ask for a way out. Other dimensions of prayer can deepen our spiritual life and make room for His will to be done. When we take time to praise and worship Him, to thank Him, to wholeheartedly repent, and to affirm our commitment to obedience and trust; our struggles begin to turn into opportunities. Our disappointments dissolve into divine appointments. And our hearts begin to see the world from God's perspective instead of our own. Our prayers begin to change *us*, reflecting His heart. Our love for Him becomes intimate, and our lives for Him become fruitful.

Jesus's public ministry was powered by His private times spent pouring His heart out to God. His circumstances didn't change when He asked His Father "to take this cup from me." Rather, He was strengthened to fulfill God's purpose for His life. Next time you sit down to pray, stay within the margins of *His* will. Don't focus on what God can do for you. Focus on what you can do for God. Grow in grace and knowledge, preparing the way for Jesus, and rejoice in His presence forever!

"The one thing I ask of the Lord-the thing I seek most- is to live in the house of the Lord all the days of my life, delighting in the Lord's perfections and meditating in his Temple" (Psalm 27:4, NLT)

12 Words

God's will is often more challenging, yet
more simplistic than our own.

Make Today Count

We were several weeks late celebrating her birthday. She had been sick. I had been out of town. But we had finally sat down at the table to acknowledge her precious life. She was weak, so we had taken a wheelchair—something she was fiercely against, but her body was rebelling—and if we were to celebrate by eating out, that is the way it would have to be.

It was there at the table that she asked me about salvation. She was afraid she would die soon, and doubtful that she was good enough to get to heaven. I sat in silence for a moment, then deflected her question. I didn't have the courage to face the truth that she was dying. And I didn't have the confidence to share my faith. My walk with God at that point had been shallow, and I wasn't prepared for discussions. I was scared that I would say something wrong, so I brushed off her comments, thinking there was plenty of time to talk. Plenty of time for me to think about what I should say. Three weeks later, as I sat at her funeral, I wept. Not only for the loss of my friend, whom I loved dearly, but also for my lack of faith. I had failed God greatly. He had been good to me, and I had abandoned His child in need. But most of all, I had failed my friend. I had failed to share the only hope that could bring her peace in her last days.

It brings me comfort to know that God is sovereign and the author of salvation. He alone, without our help, can do what he wants to accomplish. When we seek Him with all our whole hearts, we will find Him. And I believe that Melba was seeking Him whole-heartedly. But He also brings us the opportunities to share. When those opportunities arise, our obedience brings blessings—blessings of peace and love and hope. But we both missed these blessings that day because of my faithless fear. I wish I had known then, what I know now—that He did not give us a spirit of timidity, but a spirit of power and love (2 Timothy 1:7), and we can overcome our faithless fear with confident courage.

I am also assured that all of us are good enough through Christ. He wore a crown of thorns so we could wear our crown of victory. We don't have to be perfect to accept his grace. When we respond to Him with open and repentant hearts, we can be doubtlessly assured that we are, indeed, good enough.

I never got the chance to talk with Melba again. She was wheeled into surgery and never regained consciousness. But I hope, from the bottom of my heart, that she heard God's call while she lay in the hospital for three weeks, surrounded by family and friends. As we sang hymns and said prayers, I could only pray that her heart received the good news that she was good enough and that she now wears her crown of victory.

Don't ever be afraid to share what God has done for you. He will always bring you the words to say when you release your fears to faith. Don't put off until tomorrow what you can say today because tomorrow may never come.

"Always be prepared to give an answer to everyone who asks you to give a reason for the hope that you have" (1 Peter 3:15).

12 Words

Be bold and be confident. Tomorrow may
never come. Make today count!

Rabbit Holes

I had never seen a rabbit burrowed in the ground until I moved to the country. What a shock it was when I was walking one day, and the ground suddenly came flying out in front of me in the form of a rabbit! I was literally knocked to my knees as my dog on her leash took off after him. I've heard that while rabbits rest in their little hiding places, they sleep with their eyes open, always aware of predators invading their space.

We, like rabbits, have the tendency to burrow up and sleep with our eyes open. We hide from the many things in this life that cause us pain. We are constantly aware of our need to let go to the point we sometimes can't sleep. It is so much easier to hide in the things we are comfortable with than to confront the wounds that drive us underground.

I, too, hid behind my pain for way too long. There were voids in my heart that I thought gambling could fill. And even though my eyes were always open to the internal turmoil of guilt and shame, gambling had become my hiding place. And the sad thing is what I thought was comfort, was really a path to destruction.

And then one day, God showed up. Just as the rabbit jumped out in front of me, God encountered me so unexpectantly that I had no choice but to fall on my knees. Through the powerful Words of Isaiah, He opened my eyes to a new place to hide. A place that was free from guilt or shame. And soon, instead of gambling, I was hiding in His Word. I found myself rejoicing in His presence and yearning for more of His comforting grace. And now, although I'll always have a void in my life, I no longer have to hide from my pain. I am able to sing His praises, because He has filled that void with purpose and peace. He rescued me from destroying myself. He will do the same for you.

In God's presence, we find the fullness of joy. We can sprint from our burrows with the freedom to run the race that He intends for us to run, and we can peacefully close our eyes, knowing that in Him, we have a place of sheltered rest.

"You are my hiding place; you will protect me from trouble and surround me with songs of deliverance" (Psalm 32:7)

12 Words

What we think is comfort may actually be our path to destruction.

Morning Glories

We transplanted some bushes to the back corner of our yard, and every several weeks, we look out and have morning glories blooming out the top. We have never been able to find the root of the vine, but we laboriously unravel as much of the vine as we can, attempting to keep the bushes from being overtaken. But the vine is persistent and continues to return, radiating its glory in the morning.

Just like our vine, the root of our Faith may never be found by some. For a few, there is just no need for God. While yet others may have a spark of curiosity, but they don't want their faith to overtake their freedom to live without change. Even as believers, we can get so involved in life that we unravel our relationship with God because there is not enough time for Scripture and prayer.

But just as the vine continues to return on our bush, God continues to pursue us all! He never gives up on the one who rejects Him. He never lets go of the one who pushes Him aside. His love is so great for us that He sacrificed His son, and He will never abandon us, no matter how far we run or how bad we sin.

God created us for His glory, yet "we all have sinned and fall short of that glory. But God, in his grace, freely makes us right in his sight" (Romans 3:23–24, paraphrased).

Whether you are just getting to know God or have known Him for a long time, His Glory awaits! Go ahead and search for the root of the vine. Allow Him to entangle your heart. And watch in amazement as He radiates His beauty through you.

"I am the vine; you are the branches. If you remain in me and I in you, you will bear much fruit; apart from me you can do nothing" (John 15:5)

12 Words

God makes no mistakes. He pursues those
He loves. That includes you!

Oak of Righteousness

I love my beautiful oak tree. When we bought our house, it was a freebie. We were not supposed to have an extra tree, and honestly, I almost had it removed because I saw so many problems with where it was placed. Today however, my tree stands strong and majestic, and I am forever changed because of my free tree!

We have all heard Isaiah's words from God, "For my thoughts are not your thoughts, neither are your ways my ways." And little did I know, that this gift from our home builder, was actually, a gift from God.

As we became accustomed to our new home, I began to spend time under this little bitty Oak tree. I would sit and ponder and worry and doubt and mourn. I mourned the absence of a family to fill this wonderful house, this beautiful yard, and this fortunate life that we lived. The void in my heart began to grow and the bitterness began to brew. Soon, the tree became a place of pity and anger. Yet, for some reason, I was continuously drawn to this tree each and every day.

And then one day, God met me under this tree. He sat with me. He talked with me. He cried with me. And since that day, when I exchanged my pity for His purpose, He continues to meet me and teach me, under this tree.

The trees we paid for, well, they are holding their own. But the tree that was free has flourished despite my initial rebellion. This tree has grown and matured beyond our wildest dreams. Its roots are deeply growing, and its branches are reaching to the heavens. It has many flaws, but as we prune it, it becomes more healthy and refined. This tree has a purposeful life! My plans were to get rid of this tree. But God's plans were to use this tree for me to find purpose in Him!

God's grace is free to us all. His plans are rooted in us all. We can fight and find all the reasons in the world to reject the placement of His love in our lives. Or we can find true joy, by embracing the blessings of hope that He puts before us and basking in the splendor or His love.

> To all who mourn in Israel, he will give a crown of beauty for ashes, a joyous blessing instead of mourning, festive praise instead of despair. In their righteousness, they will be like great oaks that the Lord has planted for his own glory."
> (Isaiah 61:3, NLT)

12 Words

God will use our greatest pain to bring us our greatest blessings.

Road Trips

I love to take road trips! Since my parents were teachers, we were fortunate to be able to spend summers with them. And every year, we looked forward to our annual road trip. The speed limit back then was only fifty miles per hour, and sometimes it would take us several days, but we always made it to our destination safe and sound. We usually always had bumps along the way—a flat tire, a broken-down car, or a speeding ticket—but we never gave up on reaching the place that would bring us restful bliss.

When Jacob was asleep under his ladder, God promised to be with him and watch over him. He assured Jacob that he would not leave him until He had done what He had promised. But Jacob had to do his part. He had to believe, and he had to work hard! He had to place his trust in God, and he had to be confident that God would see him through. Walking with Christ can be a hard journey! We will experience bumps and bruises along the way. Our spirits get deflated, our bodies break down, and we get impatient! But in Philippians, Paul reminds us that once we place our trust in Christ, our journey will one day be completed with heavenly rewards.

We too, are assured that the prize waiting for us at the end of our journey is far greater than any difficulty we experience in our lives. What God starts in our lives, He promises He will finish! We just have to realize our dependence on God and have faith that the blessings he promises are waiting for us. We need only to be patient and trust Him. Joy and rest *are* on the horizon. Direction is more important than speed, and God is a patient God. Don't ever give up being as patient with Him as He is with us!

"And I am certain that God, who began the good work within you, will continue his work until it is finally finished on the day when Christ Jesus returns" (Philippians 1:6, NLT).

12 Words

Don't let discouragement keep you from
God's promise of rest and royalty.

Spiritual Fitness

One mile, two miles, three miles, four. You can do it, just one more! Oh, how I miss the days of running! That adrenaline high. The early morning training on my treadmill. The five kilometers, rain or shine. Challenging myself to ignore the fact that I'm hitting the wall, to go just a little bit farther. The victory of reaching the finish line. It takes hard work and determination to be an athlete and to stay physically fit. However, the training is worth the end result.

There is another kind of training though, that is even more rewarding—spiritual training. Spending time with God, alone in His Word. Meditating. Studying. Praying. Worshipping. Praising. All these things condition our minds and our hearts to run with stamina this race called life. The more we work out, the more we begin to change. The more we change and become stronger and wiser with Him, the farther we'll run to be more like Him. Exercising with God not only makes us feel better, it also brings us the confidence to run powerfully and courageously through the marathons we face, attracting others along the way.

And just as running produces an adrenaline high, once we've experienced that spiritual high, we want to just keep going and going. There's no turning back. And there is no finish line beyond eternity.

Some of us are blessed enough to be able to maintain top physical fitness well into our later years. But for others, age and health takes its toll on our old broke down bodies. But we are never too old or too broken, for spiritual fitness! It is the only exercise program that lasts forever.

"Do not conform any longer to the pattern of this world but be transformed by the renewing of your mind. Then you will be able test and approve what God's will is—his good, pleasing and perfect will" (Romans 12:2)

12 Words

Change doesn't happen without a willingness
to work hard and be challenged.

Beautiful Thorns

Life is about relationships, and sometimes relationships can get pretty sticky. But life is too short to just walk on by. Take time to smell the roses and don't let the thorns scare you away.

Our own attitudes and actions are the core of our connections. We spend so much time concentrating on how we've been wronged that we so often destroy the things that are right. We stand by selfishly watching our friendships crumble, our marriages fail, and our families fall apart because we concentrate on the thorns instead of the roses.

We all have at least one relationship in our life that needs to be restored. God delights in restoration! He is not a self-serving God. In fact, everything He created, He created for us! Even those people who really get under our skin. Yes, God even created them! And He placed them in our lives so that we can not only bless them, but we can enjoy the blessings they have to offer us.

I personally spent many years of my life in resentment, creating barriers in one of the most important relationships in my life. And I know that I am not alone. Paul reminds us in Romans that love does no harm. And even though sometimes it's hard to find love through our emotions, it is what God asks us to do. Love and forgiveness are powerful things. Once we allow ourselves to love, we begin to see past the wounds and open the door for forgiveness. We may even find a rose on the other side. That person you've been pushing away may have an aroma more pleasant than you ever expected!

Draw strength from God when you think about the defects you see in other others and praise him for the positive things you see. Get down and dirty. Put on your work gloves and get past the thorns. Not only will this build your character and help you see this person from a different perspective, it will also bring you the sweetest fragrance of love.

"Love must be sincere. Hate what is evil; cling to what it good" (Romans 12:9).

12 Words

Give birth to beauty. Savor the pedals and look past the thorns.

The Choice is Ours

Today, I am thankful for bad choices. Did I say thankful? Yes! I praise God today and thank Him for my bad choices, because through them, I grow closer to Him. Whether it's been a choice of action or a choice of words, I am reminded of the cross. They remind me of His nail scarred hands and His crown of thorns. They remind me of the suffering He took for me. They remind me that I will never be perfect, but He is perfect, and with His help, I don't have to live tied down to the regret of my choices. He reminds me that "it is finished." His perfect, unselfish love erases my imperfections, renews my Spirit, and brings me hope that next time, with His help, I'll make better choices. "The Spirit is willing, but the body is weak" (Matthew 26:41, NLT). It is only through His strength that we can resist our weaknesses. It is only through His death that we can be free. It is only through His love that we grow in His grace. But the choice is ours. We can choose to be condemned or we can choose to be complete.

"But grow in the grace and knowledge of our Lord and Savior Jesus Christ. To him be glory both now and forever! Amen" (2 Peter 3:18).

12 Words

Our bad choices don't condemn us. They
will only make us stronger!

The Bird's Nest

Several weeks after a big rain, I noticed my Carolina wren had abandoned her nest in my bird house. Since her babies weren't old enough to fly, I became worried about them. So I started digging through the nest that was left behind. There were branches and leaves, feathers and yarn, grass and trash. And not to forget, a snakeskin! Mama bird had taken all these things we might consider junk, and carefully knit them together creating a palace for her babies' new life.

I wondered if mama bird had any help building her nest, or if she did this all on her own. It amazes me that this little bitty bird could be so motivated. I think of the patience she had to have to search out her junk, squeeze it into a little bitty hole and pack it all together without anything but her wings, her feet, and her beak.

We too, have junk in our lives that can be used to make a palace. But are we as motivated as mama bird to identify that junk and turn it into something beautiful? I'm not talking about the junk that's sitting in your garage waiting to go to the dump. Or the junk that's in your closet needing to be cleaned out. I'm talking about the junk that seizes your mind and rots in your heart. The junk resulting from abuse and bitterness, depression and pain, anger and unforgiveness. The junk that makes your life miserable and detaches you from the abundance of joy that God promises.

We tend to put God in a box, thinking it's impossible to let go of our junk. But with God all things are possible! We are not expected to do it alone, and nothing is too much for Him to handle. He is compassionate and merciful, and He is waiting for you! Give God a chance and let Him unpack your most undesirable junk and turn it into your greatest treasure! Your new life awaits!

Since you have heard about Jesus and learned the truth that comes from him, throw off your old sinful nature and your former way of life, which is corrupted by lust and deception. Instead, let the Spirit renew your thoughts and attitudes. Put on your new nature, created to be like God--truly righteous and holy. (Ephesians 4:21–24, NLT)

12 Words

Our junk can be powerfully used as a treasure for God's kingdom.

The Devil Made Me Do It

The devil made me do it! This is the oldest excuse in history, going way back to when Eve blamed the devil for her own bad choice. Satan's influence certainly can be blamed for much of the evil in this world, but we as believers, don't have to use that excuse. We are equipped and empowered with the armor of God, and when we train ourselves to use it properly, we can stand against anything the devil throws our way. The devil will try to fool us into thinking that he has great power. But we must remember that he does not. Only God is omnipotent! And when we utilize the power that we have in Christ and keep our sword sharpened, we have a fighting chance to win the everyday battles we face.

Our struggles are not against flesh and blood and neither are our weapons a part of this world (2 Corinthians 10:4). We have been given the shield of faith, the helmet of salvation, and the sword of the Spirit to fight with, but it's up to us to use them.

"Now faith is being sure of what we hope for and certain of what we do not see" (Hebrews 11:1). Faith is one of our greatest gifts, and it is the means by which we come into a right relationship with God, "For it is by grace you have been saved through faith" (Ephesians 2:8). Having faith is saying "I believe in the saving Power and Hope of Christ and I will trust God and His promise." The shield of faith protects you from getting burned by the flaming arrows of deceit, fear, and doubt by firmly believing that what God has to offer is more desirable than the whispers of the devil.

God's work in us began on the cross was acknowledged when we first believed. And will continue until the day our bodies are completely restored. We can be confident in our salvation and that nothing we do will ever separate us from His love. Our helmet is our assurance that once we are saved, we are saved. Don't ever let the devil make you doubt that because you messed up, you are eternally separated from Christ! That is simply untrue. He continues to mold us, shape us, forgive us and encourage us even when we fail. "And I am certain that God, who began the good work within you, will continue his work until it is finally finished on the day when Jesus Christ returns" (Philippians 1:6, NLT).

"For the Word of God is alive and powerful. It is sharper than a two-edged sword" (Hebrews 4:12, NLT). The Word of God is the sword of the Spirit and our most powerful weapon, in pushing back the devil as he attempts to overtake us. But as with any weapon, if we aren't familiar with it and don't properly maintain it, we can't effectively use it. Meditation, memorization, and deliberate reflection of the Bible will fill our minds and our hearts with God's Truth. His Word renews us, challenges us, strengthens us, restores us, and guides us into victory when we are consumed with the battles of this world.

"Be self-controlled and alert. Your enemy the devil prowls around like a lion looking for someone to devour. Resist him, standing firm in your faith" (1 Peter 5:8). When you put on your armor of God, you say *no* to the face of the devil. You are telling the enemy that he must penetrate the power of God to get to your heart and your mind. You will resist his temptations and not fall apart, because the power that Christ has in us is greater than the power that the enemy has in the world. Be assured, you are not fighting the battle alone!

12 Words

Quit making excuses! Take up your armor,
stand firm, and rise victorious!

Hidden Treasures

We lived in our house for seventeen years before deciding to move. We were moving from the east side, which was a rough neighborhood, so I had hidden my valuables in places unseen, usually on a shelf under other things. In the back of my mind, I knew they were there; but because I hadn't had a need for them, they stayed hidden on the shelf until we moved.

Shortly before we left, I had a bout with a deep depression. I had fought minor depression before, but I didn't understand why I couldn't pull myself out of this. I went to bed with a big hole in my heart and woke up with an even bigger one. I felt like nothing would ever make the darkness go away, and I would never be myself again. In the back of my mind, I knew that God was there; but He was way up on a shelf somewhere, and I just couldn't find Him. But then one day, I fell to my knees. I cried out to Him and asked for His help. After, the day unfolded in ways that are divinely unexplainable. Instead of going to bed with a hole in my heart, I sat on the couch with a book in my hand telling me how much God loved me. My broken heart didn't go away immediately, but I started seeing light at the end of the tunnel. More importantly, I learned of God's goodness and sovereign power. It was a few years after that before I completely cleaned off that shelf and began to see what abundant life is *really* about—a healed life feasting on His promises of joy, love and peace. But most importantly, it's a life that rejoices in a personal relationship with God.

We get so caught up in how important we are and controlling our own lives that we put God on a shelf. We don't seem to have a need for him when we are doing things our own way. But God is right there! He is knocking at our door, and He wants to come in.

"He is gracious and compassionate, slow to anger and abounding in love." But we can't really know Him, until we really need Him. There is not one person that is disqualified from God's grace! He is loving, patient, and forgiving. And even though we take His love for granted, He is willing to share His feast with us. Can you hear him knocking? Open the door. Take Him off the shelf and dust Him off. Underneath you'll find your hidden treasure.

"Here I am! I stand at the door and knock. If anyone hears my voice and opens the door, I will come in and eat with him, and he with me" (Revelation 3:20).

12 Words

There's always room at His table! Indulge in the feast that awaits!

What is Your Story?

"This is my story, this is my song, praising my savior, all the day long!"[18] Who remembers this beautiful hymn by Frances J. Crosby?

We all have stories to tell, and who doesn't like a good story! As I was sitting with some friends one night, we began to share stories about our wild and crazy days. You know, those days before we had a relationship with Christ? The good ole days, the fun days, the days when we were happy, yet never fulfilled. The days where we would focus more on our own selfish wants than on what our Lord wanted of us.

As we started comparing our old lives to our new lives, we realized how much more we have now, being "filled with His goodness and lost in His love." We realized how His love has become as natural and routine in our daily lives and conversations as our selfish wants had become back then. Isn't God good?

Christ's witness is powerful and beautiful, and just as it changed our lives, it can change the lives of others as well. In fact, Jesus commands us to be wise stewards of our story when he asks us to "make disciples of all nations" (Matt 28:19). Our story, when we are willing to share, brings into focus what God is doing in our lives and what He can do in others. It brings a life-changing message of hope that brings victory over death.

Making disciples starts with relationship. A relationship with Christ and a relationship with others. Every day, you can influence those around you by modeling the actions of our Lord. Once a relationship is established, it opens the door for teaching, correcting, and building on the foundations Christ has built in us.

Are you willing to embrace the mission that Jesus gave us to make disciples? You may think that making disciples is hard. After all, it's a Biblical command that sounds a little intimidating. But it's really just as easy as sharing your story of what Christ did for you through casual conversation.

Pray today for the desire, the willingness, and the courage to share your story, making new disciples of Christ and forever friends!

"They overcame him by the blood of the Lamb and the words of their testimony" (Revelation 12:11).

12 Words

It is God's job to save, but it's our job to share.

For Better or Worse

For better or worse. Reflecting on my blessings, I give thanks for the better things in my life, but also for the worst. Our blessings don't just come to us served on a silver platter. In fact, some of our greatest blessings come from the turmoil, the pain, the suffering, and the lowest moments of our life.

God is a God of love, compassion, mercy, and justice. And sometimes life just isn't fair! It's during those times that we often accuse God of not living up to our expectations. We doubt His love, and we doubt our blessings. But those are the times we should embrace! Those are the seasons of life when we experience His love, His compassion, His mercy, and His justice in the most powerful ways. Yes, it's in the midst of the worst that His best is being done. Those are our true blessings!

So today I pray and give thanks for the good and the bad. I pray for those who see no good on the horizon, to reach out their hand to a loving and compassionate Father who will mercifully free them by way of peace. His peace that passes all understanding. I pray for those who are lonely and afraid to see the beauty of companionship through His Living Spirit. And I pray that each and every one of us, whether we're sailing along or fighting the waves, sees our blessings through the lens of God —for better or worse.

"Shall we accept good from God, and not trouble?" (Job 2:10)

12 Words

Blessings are matters of perspective. View life from the lens of God.

Precious Time

Time is such a funny thing. It is the measure we use for reaching our goals and there never seems to be enough of it. There is always much to do, so we pack our days full of obligations and plans, moving from one thing to the next, fighting for the energy to finish the race. Do you ever look back at the end of the day and wonder where it all went? What did I really accomplish? Where was the joy?

Goals are important and so is time management. Otherwise, we completely lose track of where we are and what we are hoping to accomplish. But we mustn't forget to make time for our spiritual growth as well.

One of the most precious parts of my day is the time I get to spend with the Lord. It hasn't always been that way. I have such a hard time shutting off my mind to my to-do list and being still to give praise to and worship my Father. But I've learned to schedule that time into my day. Not because it's just another obligation. But because it is the most important relationship in my life. When I don't take time to love on Him and let Him love on me, my days fly by without a glimpse of joy. He brings me energy. He brings me grace. He brings me the peace of knowing that what I don't accomplish today will still be there tomorrow.

Setting aside some undivided time for worship, study, prayer, and praise will likely become the most productive time you spend each day. And before you know it, you'll begin to see your joy increase and your stress decrease. Be still and know that He is God. It's the best use of time you'll ever spend.

"My days are swifter than a runner, they fly away without a glimpse of joy" (Job 9:25).

12 Words

Greater joy can be found. Time's too
precious to spend without God.

Was Ten Minutes Enough

W as ten minutes enough? The past three weeks had been a whirlwind. We had been overwhelmed with the unfamiliar, and life had been interrupted. When my husband's dad became ill, it was a roller coaster of ups and downs; a mission trip aborted, life altering decisions to be made, multiple four-hour trips back and forth. The love of our family kept us coasting, but even so, something was missing. It wasn't until the night of visitation that we realized what it was—the value of our relationships back home. We looked up to see the familiar faces of our friends from church. Even though they only stayed ten minutes, it was our lesson that love places no limits on time or location. You see, our friends had driven eight hours round trip and spent forty-five minutes in line, to love on us for *ten* minutes! There was no greater sacrificial love that brought us more joy and comfort during our time of grief than that short visit from our friends.

The body of Christ in our local church is where we are taught to not just believe in Christ, but to learn how to love, to live, to serve, and to think like Christ. It is sharing life with others through connection and engagement that helps us "leave the elementary teachings about Christ and go on to maturity" (Hebrews 6:1). When we take the first steps of commitment to a body of Christ, the beauty of Christ begins to reveal itself.

When building a house, a solid foundation isn't built overnight and neither is maturing in Christ. And it certainly doesn't happen just by joining a church. Maturing in Christ is a personal and corporate, life-long commitment of study, fellowship, prayer, and reflection.

That ten minutes spent with our friends is a just a fragment of the impact they had on our lives. We continue to serve together, to share life together, to learn from each other, to admonish each other, and to live life to the fullest in Christ with each other. The beauty of that ten minutes *was* enough to see Christ revealed in the reflection of our friends and to bring us the desire to move closer to Him. May God bring us all the desire for a deeper and more committed connection with Christ and with each other "*so that you may live a life worthy of the Lord and may please him in every way: bearing fruit in every good work, growing in the knowledge of God*" (Colossians 1:10).

12 Words

There's no limit to God's love. Neither should there be for ours.

Seize the Day

"Where am I going? I don't know. When will I get there? I ain't certain. All I know is I am on my way."[19] I have never seen the movie to which these words came, but this song plays in my mind all the time! These past few years have been a whirlwind of the unknown for me, but as I get up each day, I give my day to the Lord. He brings me assurance that I am on my way to accomplishing a full day of purpose. I may not know ahead of time how He will accomplish this, and I may not even know it when it happens, but my prayer is that my day will not be wasted.

In Genesis 24, Rebekah started out her day as usual. Her routine was to visit the well twice a day to draw water for her family. And on this day, she was approached by a servant of Abraham asking her for water. Rebekah, going above and beyond not only offered him water, but offered water to his camels too. All ten of them! A camel may drink up to twenty-five gallons of water a day, and water pots can be very heavy.[20] I can only imagine how exhausting it must have been to draw water for all those camels. But Rebekah served this man with joy. Little did she know that her kindness would soon bless the entire world. Because of her service to a stranger, Rebekah eventually gave birth to the father of the twelve tribes of Israel.

God can use any one of us to accomplish His greater purpose. He will use every part of our past, our present, our strengths, and our weaknesses to create not only our future, but the future of those whose lives we touch. If we fully devote our lives to Him, He will show us all we can do. Rebekah had no idea that going the extra mile for this man would become a significant part of history. And we have no idea the life changing effects our selfless acts of love can have on others.

We may not know where our lives are taking us, and we may not even know when we get there. But we do know that when we make God the center of our lives, we're on our way to beautiful places, here on earth and in eternity. He has so many blessings in store for us. So go that extra mile. Not because you have to but because you want to. Begin to make a habit of going beyond yourself in the things you do each day. The little act of kindness that you extend today could be the blessing poured out tomorrow for you and future generations.

So seize the day! Don't let any opportunity pass you by. For this could be the day for which you were made!

"And who knows but that you have come to your royal position for such a time as this?" (Esther 4:14)

12 Words

God will use your readiness to fulfill His greater purpose. Be willing!

Guarded Words

Y ou have the right to remain silent. Anything you say can and will be used against you in a court of law. You have the right to speak with an attorney and to have one present during questioning.[21]

These are the rights of our land. Our words are so powerful that we have the right not to use them for self-implication. We have the right to have counsel to help us choose our words carefully as to protect our freedom in the way they are spoken.

What if we choose our words as carefully in the best interest of others rather than just for our own protection? What if when we spoke, we spoke boldly and courageously for Christ? And what if we asked our divine counselor for guidance every time we opened our mouth?

There is power in the words we speak and there is power in God's Word. We can use our words to tear down and destroy, or we can use God's Word to encourage and build up. We can use our words to fuel the flames of our selfish desires, or we can use God's Words to ignite peace. We can choose to remain silent, or we can tell of God's abundant grace.

What words will you choose?

"Take control of what I say, O Lord, and guard my lips" (Psalm 141:3, NLT).

12 Words

Your words should bring glory and honor to God. Use them wisely.

God's Discipline

Discipline sounds like such a harsh word, especially when talking about it coming from God. We like to camp out on words like love, compassion, and peace when we reference our great and mighty God. But for us to truly understand how our lives should reflect who He is and what He calls us be, we must first humble ourselves enough to recognize where we fail. Many times, this is a painful process as we look inward and acknowledge the ugliness in our own hearts. But God is gracious and forgiving and will usually bless the mess we've created when we allow Him to correct us and show us a better way than our own. I challenge you today to listen when that little voice whispers in your heart, be willing to make adjustments in your behavior and actions, and see to it that no one, especially you, misses the grace, reverence, and awesomeness of our God.

"No discipline is enjoyable while it is happening—it's painful! But afterward there will be a peaceful harvest of right living for those who are trained in this way" (Hebrews 12:11, NLT).

12 Words

Humility is the key to usefulness and
purpose. Dispose of your pride.

The Birds and a Squirrel

I love my birds! Feeding them, watching them play, and listening to their songs of joy keeps my heart happy. They don't waste any time nourishing themselves when I fill up their cup with food. My squirrel however, shows up when the feeder is empty. She struggles for a while picking at the remnants then out of desperation, destroys my food bin to feast on the good stuff inside. As I find this very maddening, it also reminds of God's love. The squirrel knows where to find her food, but she waits until she's famished before she seeks her feast. We too, are sometimes like my squirrel. We get busy in our daily lives and forget to harvest the good words that God provides to keep us refreshed and alive. We often wait until we are empty before we rummage for His comforting food of life. But if we commit ourselves to time in His Word and connect with Him daily, we can trust in his fulfilling grace to carry us through our most destitute times.

I pray that you are all able to feast on His Words each and every day, applying it faithfully, and filling your heart with sustaining and delightful cuisine.

"Why spend money on what is not bread, and your labor on what does not satisfy? Listen, listen to me, and eat what is good, and your soul will delight in the richest of fare" (Isaiah 55:2).

12 Words

Dig in! Spiritual food is nourishment for our heart, mind, and soul.

Sticks and Stones

Sticks and stones may break my bones, but words will never hurt me![22] How many times did we say that as kids when we were offended by harsh words. At that time, it was a good come back to someone who had hurt us. But often, words will do much more damage that stones ever could.

Physical scars heal quickly, but emotional scars last forever. And getting through those emotional scars might take a long time.

Just as our actions can be examples of our faith in Christ, our words are so much more. Our words are reflections of our heart, and our hearts aren't always seeking what's best for others. We are human, so we want our thoughts to be heard. But we are also Christians. And if we don't affect the lives of those around us positively with the love of Christ, we are wasting the flavorful seasoning that we have been given.

It is hard sometimes to find that perfect balance between too much and not enough. Salt must be used in moderation. It can add flavor, but it can also ruin an opportunity to enjoy a flavorful feast. And our words, just as salt, must be used in moderation too. They can be appetizing, or they can be repulsive.

Take time to stop and think before you speak. Are your words going to bring life? Or are they going to destroy?

"Let me tell you why you are here. You're here to be salt-seasoning that brings out the God-flavors of this earth. If you lose your saltiness, how will people taste godliness?" (Matthew 5:13, MSG)

12 Words

Words reveal the flavor of our hearts. Are
ours worth second helpings?

Powdered Donuts

Powdered donuts make everything better! We really didn't need anything better than going fishing with Dad. But we stopped anyway and bought the biggest bag of powdered donuts I've ever seen! I don't even remember if we caught any fish that day, but I do know that we ate every last sprinkle in that bag.

Spending time with Dad was priceless. Though a fish or two would have been nice, the precious sprinkles of love and laughter was more than enough for this little girl.

How often do we miss the powdered donuts in life? "The thief comes only to kill, steal and destroy," and he wants more than anything to divert our attention away from the good things. We tend to look for big fish and aren't satisfied until we catch one.

But we can experience contentment in everything. Like the sprinkles of powdered donuts, our Father wants us to find joy in all aspects of life. He gives us a taste of wisdom, insight, and understanding, and He sprinkles us with His love, in many unexpected ways. He can turn the ordinary into treasures of eternal value when we savor the little sprinkles from His hand.

We sometimes think this life is all we have, but He has set eternity in our hearts and we cannot fathom what He has done from beginning to end.

And eternity begins right now. Spend some time with God, your Father, and cherish His sprinkles of grace. They are priceless and just a taste of what He has in store for you. "Taste and see that the Lord is good" (Psalm 34:8). The best is yet to come!

"He has made everything beautiful in its time. He has also set eternity in the human heart; yet no one can fathom what God has done from beginning to end" (Ecclesiastes 3:11).

12 Words

You can't produce the taste of God. It's something you must acquire.

Incidental Dreams

I remember those days, many years ago, when I would crank up my rock-n-roll records, get out my air guitar and hairbrush microphone, and sing my little heart. I fantasied, as most kids do, of being rich and famous. I dreamed that one day, I too, might be on stage in front of thousands of people, making music of my own.

Now, anyone who really knows me, or who has ever heard me sing, knows that it's probably best that I don't get on stage and do anything! But nevertheless, I dreamt big and often would pray that God would make all my dreams come true.

Let me start by saying that nothing is too big for God. Never give up on your dreams! Hard work, determination, obedience, and faith can make any dream come true. He is capable of doing more than we could ever imagine. *So don't ever quit.*

I am reminded though, that *our* dreams may not be the plans that God has for us. God has a plan for each of us and wants what is best for us. And He doesn't need us to be rich and famous to achieve His best. He needs us to be willing and able.

God doesn't promise that we'll be materially prosperous in this life, but he does promise to meet our deepest needs. He doesn't promise to give us everything we want, but He will also not withhold anything that is inherently good. We can get so focused on who we are not, and what we have not, that we lose sight of whose we are and what we are called to do.

We often pray that God will lead us to the next step of making our dreams come true. But how often do we pray for God to use us where we are at? How often do we say, "I am satisfied Lord with what I have and who I am. Take me and use me for your glory." How often do we allow His Word and His Presence to genuinely satisfy our soul?

What I am realizing is that God is making my dreams come true, but they are not the dreams I created myself. I have come to realize that even the dreams I had of fame and fortune, don't come close to the satisfaction that I have in God's promises. He meets my deepest need by loving me, forgiving me, and giving me a purpose in life. He satisfies me as with the richest of foods, so I can sing praises to Him (Psalm 63:5).

Start the day off by asking God to use you where you are. Be satisfied with what you have and where you are at and use it for His glory today!

"Delight yourself in the Lord and he will give you the desires of your heart" (Psalm 37:4).

12 Words

When your focus is on living for Christ,
your dreams become incidental.

Son Rise

Our family vacations consisted of getting up in the wee hours of the morning and heading off to somewhere fun. Our day always began with a bet from Dad—what time would the sun rise? It wasn't until I was old enough to comprehend the newscast that I figured out why he always won! But nonetheless, we always knew our trip would begin anxiously awaiting the sunrise.

As we journey through life, we too can wonder when the sun is going to rise. We get so consumed with the many things we must do and get so buried in our obligations that we can't find a way to dig ourselves out. Even vacations have become burdensome for many, because we don't make time to take time-out. In our stress, we grow tired, weak, and weary and begin to doubt what life is all about.

But there is place where the sun shines twenty-four-seven. A place where our roots become quenched and our branches begin to grow. It's a place that develops our character and brings us rest. Where even on our darkest days, we don't have to guess what time the sun will rise because He's already there. This place is a journey to the cross. Jesus will carry you day in and day out, love you like you've never been loved, and give you vision to see right through the clouds. Your mysteries will become understanding. Your days will become filled with abundance of life as you live life with Him, and for Him.

When I was a child, I saw the sun as a way to beat my Dad in a bet! But now, I see the Son as my friend. He is the light of my world, and my days have never been brighter!

It's never too late to let the Son rise on your horizon. Finding Jesus is the most beautiful journey you will ever take, and the most peaceful destination you could ever hope to look forward to.

When I was a child, I spoke and thought and reasoned as a child. But when I grew up, I put away childish things. Now we see things imperfectly, like puzzling reflections in a mirror, but then we will see everything with perfect clarity. All that I know now is partial and incomplete, but then I will know everything completely, just as God now knows me completely. (1 Corinthians 13:11–12, NLT)

12 Words

God's just as interested in our journey, as He is our destination.

Trust and Obey

"Trust and obey, for there's no other way, to be happy in Jesus than to trust and obey!"[23] So often I sang that song in church and it was just another song. But now, I know it's not just a song. It's a way of life! My God is such an awesome God. His provision of joy is so much more than I could have ever imagined. I only needed to place my complete trust in Him and listen to the small little voices that whisper in my heart to receive the blessings that he had in store for me. Every day, I am amazed at the joy and peace that He continues to bring me through trusting Him and obeying his callings in my life.

I haven't always been at peace or had such joy. For a season, my happiness was very challenged. My struggles of growing old and having no children depleted my value in myself as I searched for my purpose for many painful months. I was rebellious and stubborn, relying on myself to ease my pain. But God brought me to a place of resignation, bowing to his great and mighty power, and turning my sorrows into joy and my pain into heavenly pleasures.

My story is not extraordinary. It's not even unique. Many women walk through life alone, afraid of the future. My story however is a journey of grace and victory; a journey of trust and obedience and accepting the path where God is leading me. It's a journey of welcoming my Father's grace and yielding to His love. A journey of healing and renewal. Through this burden, He has shaped my character. Through my insecurity, He built my confidence. Through my trust in Him, He has strengthened my faith. Through my obedience, He has brought me purpose. He taught me that when I trust him, when I obey him, he will bring an unimaginable satisfaction by just being in His presence. What my earthly future holds, only He knows. But I know without a doubt, where my eternal future lies.

My prayer for you is that you will find the same peace and the same joy that I have found by trusting and obeying my Father and my Friend.

12 Words

Obedience is the one thing in life that only we can control.

Benediction

I hope you have enjoyed these devotions and have taken time to absorb the truths of each one. I pray that if you don't walk away with any other truth, it's the one truth that you are loved by a merciful and compassionate heavenly Father who created you in His image. He is enough to satisfy your every need and will provide enough to sustain you if you'll allow your full identity to reside in the unseen walls of His kingdom. He has given *you* the power to be enough, and you are worth it!

> Brothers, and sisters, think of what you were when you were called. Not many of you were wise by human standards; not many were influential; not many were of noble birth. But God chose the foolish things of the world to shame the wise; God chose the weak things of the world to shame the strong. God chose the lowly things of this world and the despised things—and the things that are not—to nullify the things that are, so that no one may boast before him. It is because of him that you are in Christ Jesus, who has become for us wisdom from God-that is, our righteousness, holiness, and redemption. (1 Corinthians 1:26-30,[24] New NIV)

12 Words

The world may see worthless. But God
sees esteemed. You are enough!

Endnotes

1   Unless otherwise noted, all Scripture are referenced from the *New International Life Application Study Bible* (Grand Rapids, MI: Zondervan, 1984).

2   Dr. Scott Sharman, Alsbury Baptist Church, Burleson, Texas.

3   Binion's Horseshoe Casino128 Fremont St, Las Vegas, NV 89101

4   Dictionary.com 2018 iPhone app (Apple App Store)

5   Dictionary.com 2018 iPhone app (Apple App Store)

6   Dictionary.com 2018 iPhone app (Apple App Store)

7   This report was unverifiable. It was a picture posted on multiple Facebook pages but not ever any media outlet or articles attached to it (May 19, 2016).

8   Peter Scholtes, *They'll Know We are Christians*, 1966.

9   Co-written by my dear friend Rolanda Hairston.

10   Deitrich Bonhoeffer, *The Cost of Discipleship* (New York: Macmillan, 1959).

11   Unless otherwise noted, all NLT Scripture are referenced from the *Contemporary Comparative Side-by-Side Bible* (Grand Rapids, MI: Zondervan, 2011).

12   Dictionary.com

13   Bobby McFerrin, released September 1988

14   Unless otherwise noted, all GNB Scripture are referenced from the *You Version app by Bible.com*

15   Unless otherwise noted, all NKJV Scripture are referenced from the *Contemporary Comparative Side-by-Side Bible* (Grand Rapids, MI: Zondervan, 2011).

16   Unless otherwise noted, all AMP Scripture are referenced from the *You Version app by Bible.com*

17 William D. Barney, *Words from a Wide Land* (Denton, TX: University of North Texas Press, 1993). 10

18 Fanny Crosby and Phoebe Knapp, *"Blessed Assurance"*, a Christian hymn, 1873

19 Alan Jay Lerner and Frederick Loewe, *Paint Your Wagon (I'm on my Way)*, 1969

20 *New International Life Application Study Bible*, (Grand Rapids, MI: Zondervan, 1984), pg 44

21 Miranda Rights, *Miranda v. Arizona*, United States Supreme Court, June 1966

22 African Methodist Episcopal Church, *Christian Recorder*, March 1862

23 John Sammis, *Trust and Obey*, 1887

24 Scripture reference from the *Contemporary Comparative Side-by-Side Bible* (Grand Rapids, MI: Zondervan, 2011).

Bibliography

African Methodist Episcopal Church. *Christian Recorder*, March 1862.

Barney, William D., *Words from a Wide Land.* Denton, TX: University of North Texas Press, 1993.

Bonhoeffer, Deitrich. *The Cost of Discipleship.* New York: Macmillan. 1959.

Crosby, Fanny and Knapp, Phoebe. *Blessed Assurance.* 1873.

Lerner, Alan Jay and Loewe, Frederick, *Paint Your Wagon (I'm on My Way).* 1969.

Miranda Rights, *Miranda v. Arizona*, United States Supreme Court, June 1966.

Sammis, John. *Trust and Obey.* 1887.

Scholtes, Peter. *They'll Know We are Christians.* 1966.

Unless otherwise noted, all NIV Scripture are referenced from the *New International Life Application Study Bible* (Grand Rapids, MI: Zondervan, 1984).

Unless otherwise noted, all NLT Scripture are referenced from the *Contemporary Comparative Side-by-Side Bible* (Grand Rapids, MI: Zondervan, 2011).

Unless otherwise noted, all NKJV Scripture are referenced from the *Contemporary Comparative Side-by-Side Bible* (Grand Rapids, MI: Zondervan, 2011).

New NIV Scripture reference is from the *Contemporary Comparative Side-by-Side Bible* (Grand Rapids, MI: Zondervan, 2011).

Unless otherwise noted, all AMP Scripture are referenced from the *You Version app by Bible.com*

Unless otherwise noted, all GNB Scripture are referenced from the *You Version app by Bible.com*

About the Author

Susan Dodson was born and raised in Fort Worth, Texas. Always possessing a gift for writing, she researched and developed guidelines and policies for the prosperous orthodontic practice she managed for twenty-seven years. After a powerful encounter with the Lord, she heard a call for something greater. Not knowing exactly what that meant, she and her husband took a leap of faith as she left her career and retired without any plans for her future

From there, God took the wheel, using her former addiction to develop her writing into spiritual devotions. She earned a Certificate of Christian Ministry from Liberty University and currently uses her business background to serve in the financial office at Alsbury Baptist Church in Burleson, Texas.

Susan has a passion for Jesus, missions, adventure, and advocacy. Her heart has planted seeds in Haiti, where she serves annually. She enjoys rattlesnake hunting in West Texas, spending hot Texas summers in the Colorado Rockies, and helping anyone in need.

CPSIA information can be obtained
at www.ICGtesting.com
Printed in the USA
FSHW021028110619

9 781645 157342